TELL ME HOW

HOW HOT?

by Azra Limbada

KidHaven PUBLISHING

Published in 2023 by **KidHaven Publishing,**
an Imprint of Greenhaven Publishing, LLC
29 East 21st Street
New York, NY 10010

© 2021 Booklife Publishing
This edition is published by arrangement with
Booklife Publishing

Edited by: William Anthony

Designed by: Danielle Webster-Jones

Cataloging-in-Publication Data

Names: Limbada, Azra.
Title: How hot? / Azra Limbada.
Description: New York : KidHaven Publishing, 2023. | Series: Tell me how | Includes glossary and index.
Identifiers: ISBN 9781534540934 (pbk.) | ISBN 9781534540958 (library bound) | ISBN 9781534540941 (6 pack) | ISBN 9781534540965 (ebook)
Subjects: LCSH: Desert animals--Juvenile literature.
Classification: LCC QL116.L563 2023 | DDC 591.754--dc23

All rights reserved. No part of this book may be reproduced in any form without permission in writing from the publisher, except by a reviewer.

Manufactured in the United States of America

CPSIA compliance information: Batch #CSKH23. For further information contact Greenhaven Publishing LLC, New York, New York at 1-844-317-7404.

Please visit our website, www.greenhavenpublishing.com. For a free color catalog of all our high-quality books, call toll free 1-844-317-7404 or fax 1-844-317-7405.

Find us on [f] [Ig]

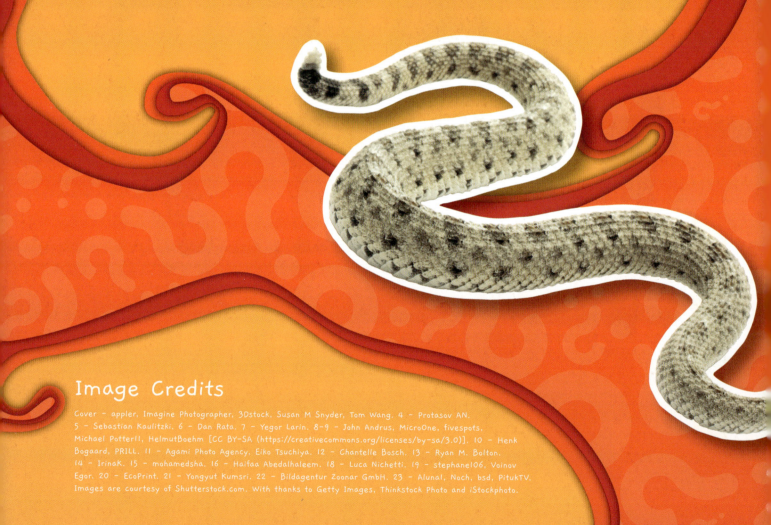

Image Credits

Cover – appler, Imagine Photographer, 3Dstock, Susan M Snyder, Tom Wang. 4 – Protasov AN. 5 – Sebastian Kaulitzki. 6 – Dan Rata. 7 – Yegor Larin. 8–9 – John Andrus, MicroOne, fivespots, Michael Potter11, HelmutBoehm [CC BY-SA (https://creativecommons.org/licenses/by-sa/3.0)]. 10 – Henk Bogaard, PRILL. 11 – Agami Photo Agency, Eiko Tsuchiya. 12 – Chantelle Bosch. 13 – Ryan M. Bolton. 14 – IrinaK. 15 – mohamedsha. 16 – Haifaa Abedalhaleem. 18 – Luca Nichetti. 19 – stephane106, Voinov Egor. 20 – EcoPrint. 21 – Yongyut Kumsri. 22 – Bildagentur Zoonar GmbH. 23 – Alunal, Noch, bsd, PitukTV. Images are courtesy of Shutterstock.com. With thanks to Getty Images, Thinkstock Photo and iStockphoto.

CONTENTS

PAGE 4   Extreme Animals

PAGE 6   Living in the Desert

PAGE 8   How Hot?

PAGE 10   Sidewinder Snake

PAGE 12   Desert Tortoise

PAGE 14   Dung Beetle

PAGE 16   Rüppell's Fox

PAGE 18   Amazing Adaptations

PAGE 20   Life in the Desert

PAGE 22   Create a Creature

PAGE 24   Glossary and Index

Words that look like **this** can be found in the glossary on page 24.

EXTREME ANIMALS

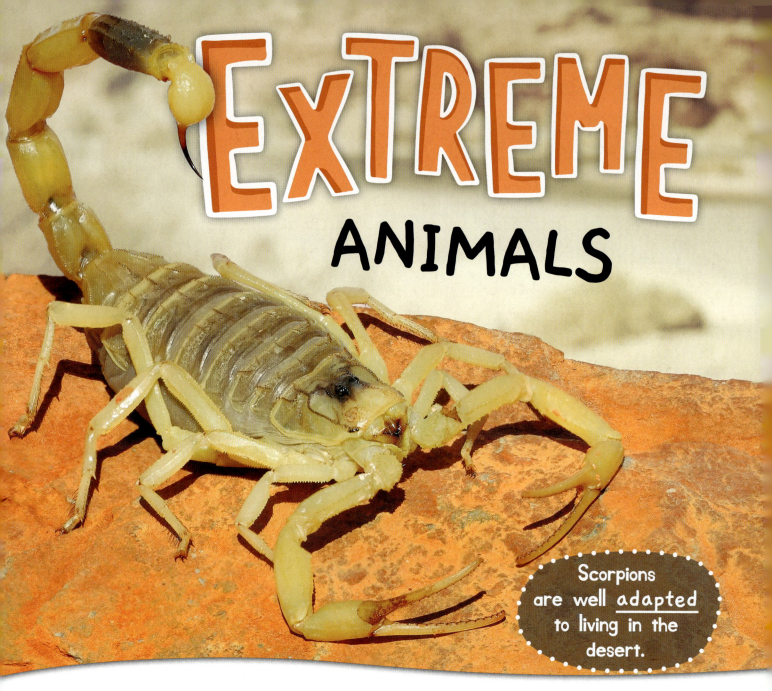

Scorpions are well <u>adapted</u> to living in the desert.

Some living things can survive in very <u>extreme</u> places. They are called extremophiles. Their homes can be very dangerous, such as in the middle of a hot desert.

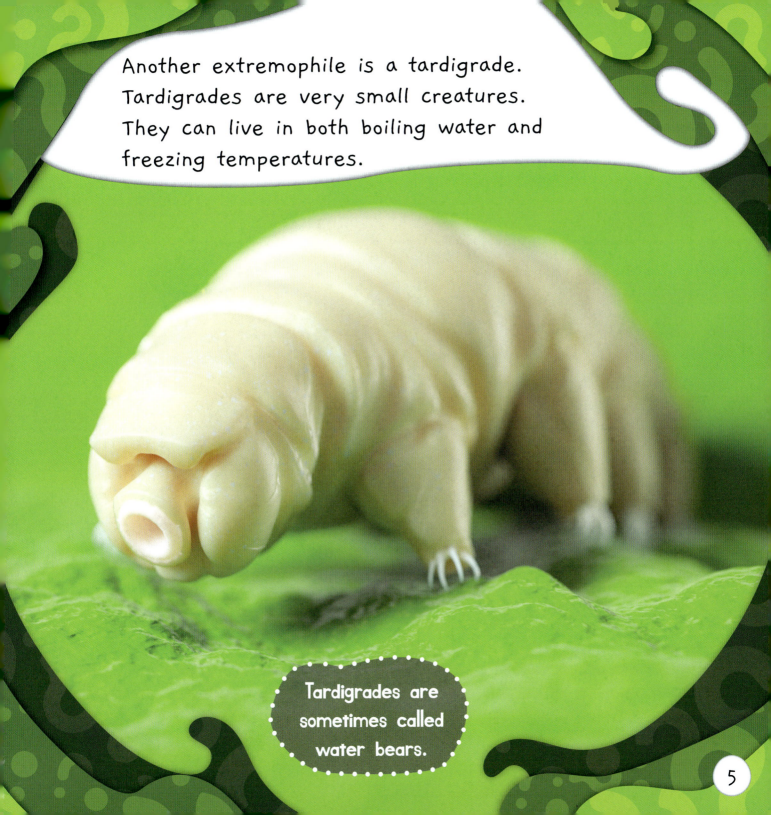

Another extremophile is a tardigrade. Tardigrades are very small creatures. They can live in both boiling water and freezing temperatures.

Tardigrades are sometimes called water bears.

LIVING IN THE DESERT

A desert is an area of land that has very little rain. Some deserts can be very hot in the day but very cold at night.

There are different types of deserts on Earth.

Did you know that a desert doesn't always have to be filled with sand? Some deserts are covered in ice, such as polar deserts. These areas also get very little rainfall.

Deserts can be sandy or icy.

HOW HOT?

Animals that live in the desert have special ways of surviving in the heat and the cold. Some are awake at night and some are awake during the day! Let's take a look at the temperatures different desert animals can live in.

RÜPPELL'S FOX
158 degrees Fahrenheit (70 degrees Celsius)

Some dung beetles are nocturnal. This means they are only awake at night. Did you know that dung beetles eat poop left behind by other animals?

DUNG BEETLE
140 degrees Fahrenheit (60 degrees Celsius)

DESERT TORTOISE
120 degrees Fahrenheit (49 degrees Celsius)

SIDEWINDER SNAKE
118 degrees Fahrenheit (48 degrees Celsius)

SIDEWINDER SNAKE

The sidewinder snake can be found in many different deserts. It does not slither forward like other snakes. Instead, it moves from side to side in the sand.

Can you see the tracks this sidewinder has made by moving sideways?

Sidewinders are nocturnal animals.

The sidewinder is a type of rattlesnake. It has small horns above each eye. The horns keep the sand out of the snake's eyes.

DESERT TORTOISE

The desert tortoise can be found in places such as the Mojave Desert in North America. Desert tortoises can live for up to 50 years!

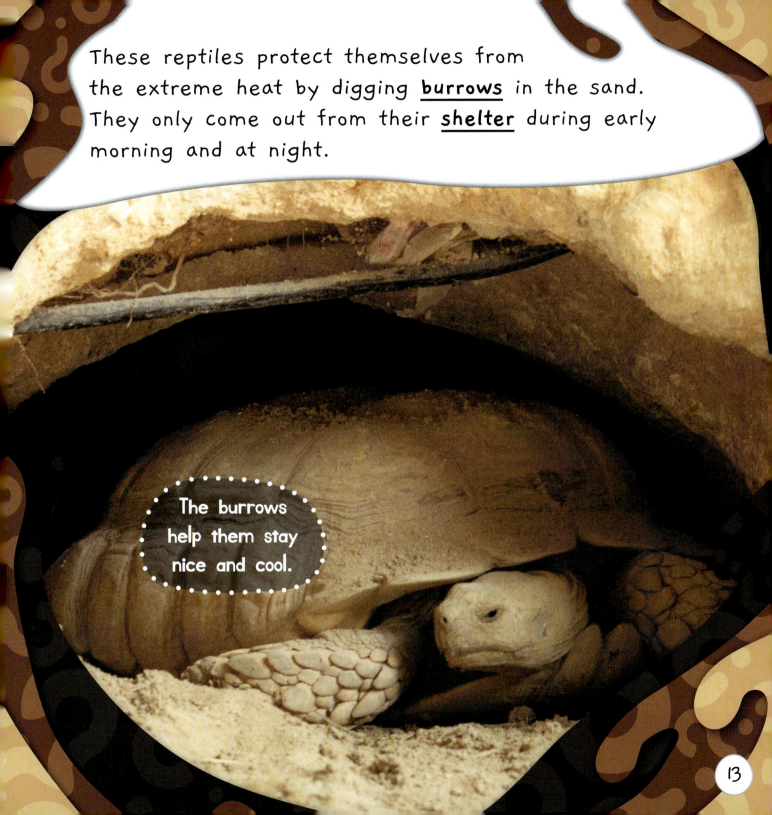

These reptiles protect themselves from the extreme heat by digging **burrows** in the sand. They only come out from their **shelter** during early morning and at night.

The burrows help them stay nice and cool.

DUNG BEETLE

Dung beetles get their food and water from poop!

Dung beetles can live almost anywhere, except in the freezing cold of Antarctica. They collect animal poop and roll it into a ball.

Nocturnal dung beetles in the Sahara use the stars in the sky to help them figure out which direction to travel in!

These beetles are also called scarab beetles.

RÜPPELL'S FOX

This little fox lives across northern Africa and parts of the Middle East, including one of the world's hottest deserts – the Lut desert. The Lut desert is in Iran.

The hottest temperature ever recorded in the Lut desert was 158 degrees Fahrenheit (70 degrees Celsius).

Rüppell's fox has fur on the pads of its paws. This helps it to walk on the hot sand without getting burned.

These foxes are also nocturnal. They come out at night to hunt.

AMAZING ADAPTATIONS

Meerkats have dark parts around their eyes that make it easier for them to see in bright sunlight.

All animals are adapted to their environment. They have certain **features** that help them survive in their **habitat**.

Camels are well adapted to their desert habitats. They have long eyelashes that keep sand and dust out of their eyes.

Long eyelashes

A camel can also go a week or more without any water!

LIFE IN THE DESERT

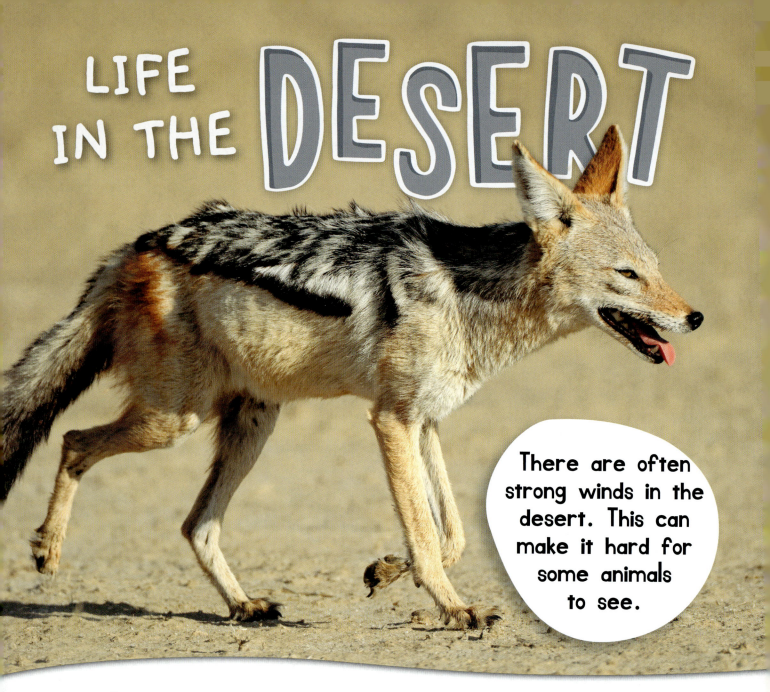

There are often strong winds in the desert. This can make it hard for some animals to see.

Life in the desert is difficult because of the extreme weather, but plenty of animals and plants have found clever ways to survive.

Deserts are not just home to animals. People live in them too! There are around 2.5 million people living in the Sahara in Africa.

Some people travel across the Sahara on camels.

CREATE A CREATURE

The thorny devil lizard can **absorb** water into its skin, which then drips down into its mouth. This helps it stay **hydrated** in the heat.

Look at how the lizard is covered in spikes!

GLOSSARY

absorb to take in or soak up

adapted changed over time to suit the environment

burrows holes or tunnels dug by an animal

extreme far beyond what is usual or normal

features interesting or important parts

habitat the natural home in which animals, plants, and other living things live

hydrated having taken in enough water or other liquid

shelter a safe place that protects an animal from the environment

INDEX

adaptations 4, 18–19, 23

deserts 4, 6–8, 11–12, 14, 16, 19–21, 23

extremophiles 4–5

habitats 18–19

night 6, 8–9, 15, 17

nocturnal animals 9, 11, 13, 17

people 21

rain 6–7

sand 7, 12–13, 15, 17, 19